CONTENTS

Tunes included in VOLUME 133 are:

Any codas (✛) that appear will be played only once
on the recording at the end of the last recorded chorus.

PLAY-A-LONG CD INFORMATION
STEREO SEPARATION: LEFT CHANNEL=Banjo, Tuba & Drums or Washboard*
RIGHT CHANNEL=Piano, Tuba & Drums or Washboard*
TUNING NOTES: Concert B♭ & A (A=440)

PERSONNEL ON PLAY-A-LONG RECORDING
BOB STEVENS - Banjo; ROGER DANE - Piano; QUENTIN SHARPENSTEIN - Tuba
BRUCE MORROW - Drums; SAM GOODSON - Washboard*

Published by
JAMEY AEBERSOLD JAZZ®
P.O. Box 1244
New Albany, IN 47151-1244
www.jazzbooks.com
ISBN 978-1-56224-287-9

Engraving
DAVID SILBERMAN

Cover Design & Layout
JASON A. LINDSEY

BOOK ONLY: $5.95 U.S.

LYRICS

1. DOWN BY THE RIVERSIDE
I'm gonna lay down my sword and shield
Down by the riverside,
Down by the riverside,
Down by the riverside.
I'm gonna lay down my sword and shield
Down by the riverside,
Down by the riverside.

Chorus:
Ain't gonna study war no more,
Ain't gonna study war no more,
Ain't gonna study war no more.
Ain't gonna study war no more,
Ain't gonna study war no more,
Ain't gonna study oh war no more.

I'm gonna talk with the Prince of Peace
Down by the riverside,
Down by the riverside,
Down by the riverside.
I'm gonna talk with the Prince of Peace

Chorus

2. SMILES
There are smiles that make us happy,
There are smiles that make us blue,
There are smiles that steal away the teardrops,
As the sunbeams steal away the dew,
There are smiles that have a tender meaning
That the eyes of love alone may see,
And the smiles that fill my life with sunshine
Are the smiles that you give to me.

3. JAZZ ME BLUES
Down in Louisiana in that sunny clime,
They play a class of music that is super fine,
And it makes no difference if it's rain or shine,
You can hear that jazzin' music playin' all the time.

It sounds so peculiar 'cause it's really queer,
How its sweet vibrations seems to fill the air,
Then to you the whole world seems to be in rhyme;
You'll want nothin' else but jazzin', jazzin' all the time.

Every one that I ever came to spy, hear them loudly cry:
Oh, jazz me!
Come on, Professor, and jazz me!
Jazz me!
You know I like my dancing both day and night,
And if I don't get my jazzin', I don't feel right,
Now if it's ragtime, take a lick, play it in jazz time,
Jazz time!
Don't want it fast, don't want it slow;
Take your time, Professor, play it sweet and low!
I got those doggone, low-down jazz-me jazz-me blues!

Jazz me!
Come on, Professor, and jazz me!
Jazz me!
You know I like my dancing both day and night,
And if I don't get my jazzin', I don't feel right,
Now if it's ragtime, take a lick, play it in jazz time,
Jazz time!
Don't want it fast, don't want it slow;
Take your time, Professor, play it sweet and low!
I got those doggone, low-down jazz-me, jazz-me blues!

4. WABASH BLUES
Oh, those Wabash Blues,
I know I got my dues.
A lonesome soul am I,
I feel that I could die.
Candle light that gleams,
Haunts me in my dreams.
I'll pack my walkin' shoes
To lose those Wabash Blues.

5. JA-DA
Ja-da, ja-da, ja-da, ja-da, jing, jing, jing.
Ja-da, ja-da, ja-da, ja-da, jing, jing, jing.
That's a funny little bit of melody.
It's so soothing and appealing to me,
It goes ja-da, ja-da, ja-da, ja-da, jing, jing, jing.

6. AVALON
I found my love in Avalon beside the bay.
I left my love in Avalon and sailed away.
I dream of her and Avalon from dusk 'til dawn,
And so I think I'll travel on to Avalon.

7. JUST A CLOSER WALK WITH THEE
Just a closer walk with Thee,
Grant it, Jesus, is my plea,
Daily walking close to Thee,
Let it be, dear Lord, let it be.

I am weak, but Thou art strong,
Jesus, keep me from all wrong,
I'll be satisfied as long
As I walk, let me walk close to Thee.

Through this world of toil and snares,
If I falter, Lord, who cares?
Who with me my burden shares?
None but Thee, dear Lord, none but Thee.

When my feeble life is o'er,
Time for me will be no more,
Guide me gently, safely o'er
To Thy kingdom's shore, to Thy shore.

8. SOME OF THESE DAYS

Some of these days you'll miss me, honey,
Some of these days you'll feel so lonely;
You'll miss my hugging, you'll miss my kissing,
You'll miss me, honey, when you're away.

I feel so lonely just for you only,
For you know, honey, you've had your way,
And when you leave me, you know 'twill grieve me;
I'll miss my little dad-dad-daddy, yes some of these days.

9. A GOOD MAN IS HARD TO FIND

A good man is hard to find,
You always get the other kind,
Just when you think that he is your pal
You look for him and find him fooling 'round some other gal,
Then you rave, you even crave
To see hem laying in his grave;
So if your man is nice
Take my advice
And hug him in the morning
Kiss him every night,
Give him plenty lovin', treat him right
For a good man nowadays is hard to find.

10. WASHINGTON & LEE SWING

When Washington and Lee's men fall in line,
We're going to win again another time;
For W&L I yell, I yell, I yell,
And for the University, I yell, like hell!
And we will fight! fight! fight! for every yard;
Circle the ends and hit that line right hard!
And we will roll those Wahoos on the sod!
Yes, by God! RAH! RAH! RAH!
HEY!

11. BALLIN' THE JACK

First you put your two knees close up tight,
Then you sway 'em to the left, then you sway 'em to the right,
Step around the floor kind of nice and light,
Then you twis' around and twis' around with all your might,
Stretch your lovin' arms straight out in space
Then do the Eagle Rock with style and grace
Swing your foot way 'round then bring it back,
Now that's what I call "Ballin' the Jack."

12. WHEN THE SAINTS GO MARCHIN' IN

Oh, when the saints go marching in
Oh, when the saints go marching in
Lord, how I want to be in that number
When the saints go marching in.

13. WHO'S SORRY NOW?

Who's sorry now?
Who's sorry now?
Whose heart is aching for breaking each vow?
Who's sad and blue?
Who's crying too?
Just like I cried over you?

Right to the end
Just like a friend
I tried to warn you somehow
You had your way,
Now you must pay
I'm glad that you're sorry now.

Right to the end
Just like a friend
I tried to warn you somehow
You had your way,
Now you must pay
I'm glad that you're sorry now.

14. CHINA BOY

China boy, go sleep,
Close your eyes, don't peep,
Sandman soon will come,
While I softly hum.

Buddha smiles on you,
Moonman loves you too;
So, while their watch they keep,
China boy, go sleep.

15. TOOT, TOOT, TOOTSIE! (GOODBYE!)

Toot, toot, Tootsie, good-bye!
Toot, toot, Tootsie, don't cry.
The choo choo train that takes me
Away from you no words can tell how sad it makes me.
Kiss me, Tootsie, and then
Do it over again, watch for the mail, I'll never fail
If you don't get a letter then you'll know I'm in jail.
Toot, toot, Tootsie don't cry
Toot, toot, Tootsie, good-bye.

1. Down By The Riverside

PLAY 6 CHORUSES (♩ = 220)

American Gospel Song

Fine

2. Smiles

PLAY 5 CHORUSES ($\quad$ = 160)

By J. Will Callahan and Lee S. Roberts

3. Jazz Me Blues

PLAY 7 CHORUSES (♩ = 216)

By Tom DeLaney

4. Wabash Blues

PLAY 3 CHORUSES ($\quad$ = 106)

By Dave Ringle and Fred Meinken

5. Ja-Da

PLAY 8 CHORUSES ($\quarternote = 174$)

By Bob Carleton

6. Avalon

By Al Jolson and B.G. DeSylva
Music by Vincent Rose

PLAY 7 CHORUSES (♩ = 250)

7. Just A Closer Walk With Thee

8. Some Of These Days

PLAY 6 CHORUSES (♩ = 212)

By Shelton Brooks

SOLOS

CODA

9. A Good Man Is Hard To Find

By Eddie Green

PLAY 4 CHORUSES (♩ = 112)

PLAY 7 CHORUSES (♩ = 280)

By Mark Sheafe, Clarence Robbins and Thornton Allen

SOLOS (on 7th chorus take 2nd ending)

11. Ballin' The Jack

11

12. When The Saints Go Marchin' In

PLAY 12 CHORUSES (♩ = 254)

American Gospel Hymn

13. Who's Sorry Now?

PLAY 5 CHORUSES (♩ = 188)
CD Tracks 13 and 16

Words by Bert Kalmar and Harry Ruby
Music by Ted Snyder

14. China Boy

PLAY 7 CHORUSES (♩= 248)
CD Tracks 14 and 17

By Dick Winfree and Phil Boutelje

14

1. Down By The Riverside

PLAY 6 CHORUSES ($\quad$ = 220)

American Gospel Song

Fine

2. Smiles

PLAY 5 CHORUSES (♩ = 160)

By J. Will Callahan and Lee S. Roberts

3. Jazz Me Blues

PLAY 7 CHORUSES (♩ = 216)

By Tom DeLaney

SOLOS

Solo Break ... PLAY

Solo Break ... PLAY

18

4. Wabash Blues

PLAY 3 CHORUSES (♩ = 106)

By Dave Ringle and Fred Meinken

SOLOS

ritard for ending _ _ _

5. Ja-Da

PLAY 8 CHORUSES (♩ = 174)

By Bob Carleton

6. Avalon

21

7. Just A Closer Walk With Thee

PLAY 4 CHORUSES ($\bullet$ = 66)

American Spiritual

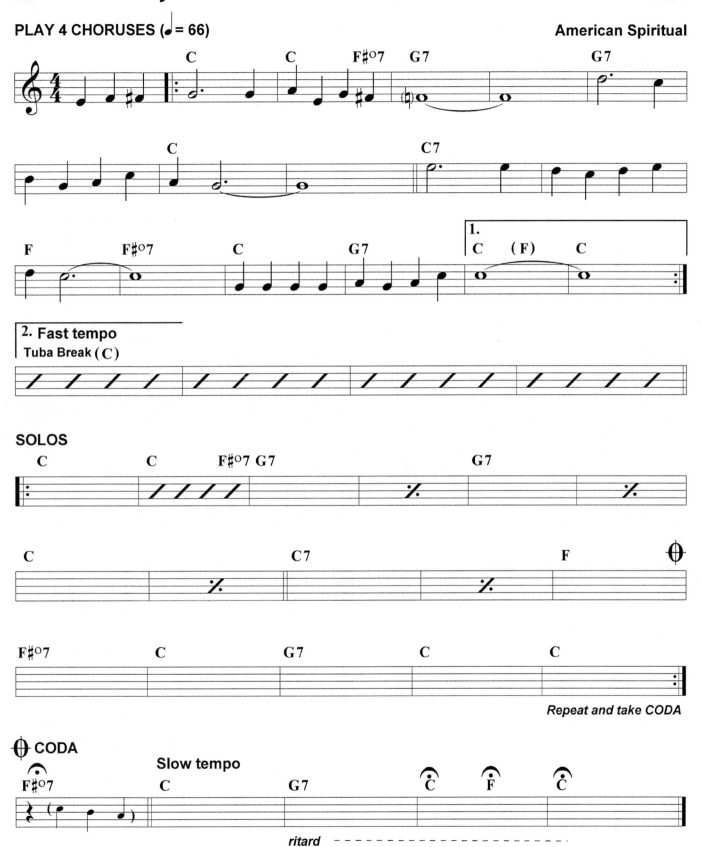

Repeat and take CODA

ritard — — — — — — — — — — — — — — — — — —

8. Some Of These Days

PLAY 6 CHORUSES (♩= 212)

By Shelton Brooks

9. A Good Man Is Hard To Find

PLAY 4 CHORUSES (♩ = 112)

By Eddie Green

10. Washington and Lee Swing

PLAY 7 CHORUSES (♩ = 280) **By Mark Sheafe, Clarence Robbins and Thornton Allen**

25

11. Ballin' The Jack

PLAY 5 CHORUSES ($\quarternote = 128$)

By Jim Burris and Chris Smith

12. When The Saints Go Marchin' In

PLAY 12 CHORUSES (♩ = 254)

American Gospel Hymn

13. Who's Sorry Now?

PLAY 5 CHORUSES (♩= 188)
CD Tracks 13 and 16

Words by Bert Kalmar and Harry Ruby
Music by Ted Snyder

28

14. China Boy

PLAY 7 CHORUSES (♩ = 248)
CD Tracks 14 and 17

By Dick Winfree and Phil Boutelje

15. Toot, Toot, Tootsie! (Goodbye!)

PLAY 5 CHORUSES (♩ = 240)
CD Tracks 15 and 18

Words and Music by Gus Kahn, Ernie Erdman,
Dan Russo, and Ted Fiorito

1. Down By The Riverside

PLAY 6 CHORUSES (♩ = 220)

American Gospel Song

SOLOS

2. Smiles

PLAY 5 CHORUSES (♩ = 160)

By J. Will Callahan and Lee S. Roberts

3. Jazz Me Blues

PLAY 7 CHORUSES (♩= 216)

By Tom DeLaney

4. Wabash Blues

PLAY 3 CHORUSES (♩ = 106)   By Dave Ringle and Fred Meinken

SOLOS

ritard for ending

34

5. Ja-Da

PLAY 8 CHORUSES (♩ = 174)

By Bob Carleton

SOLOS

CODA

6. Avalon

PLAY 7 CHORUSES (♩ = 250)

By Al Jolson and B.G. DeSylva
Music by Vincent Rose

7. Just A Closer Walk With Thee

PLAY 4 CHORUSES (♩= 66)

American Spiritual

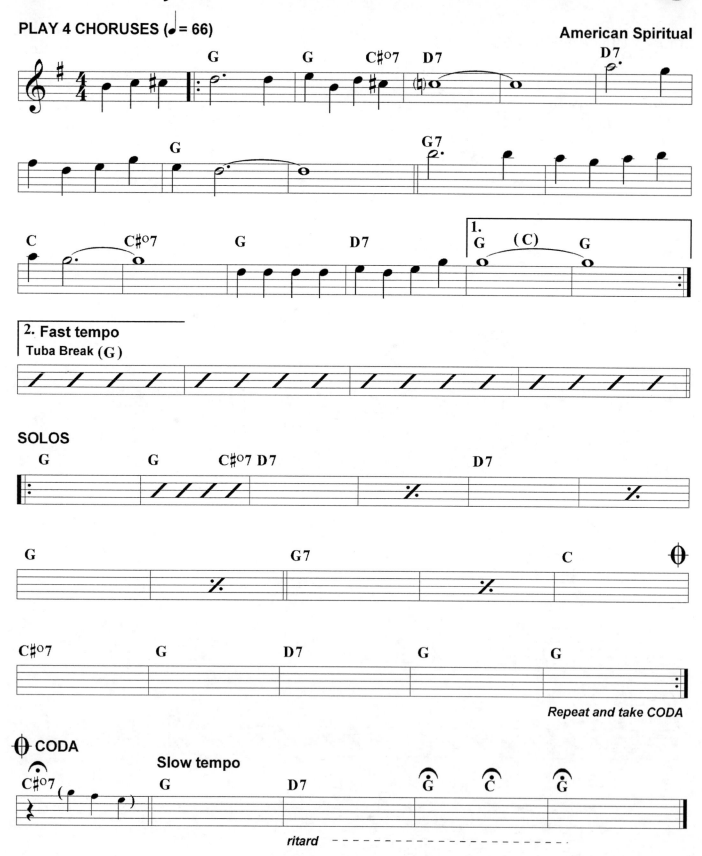

8. Some Of These Days

PLAY 6 CHORUSES (♩= 212)

By Shelton Brooks

SOLOS

CODA

9. A Good Man Is Hard To Find

PLAY 4 CHORUSES (♩ = 112)

By Eddie Green

10. Washington and Lee Swing

PLAY 7 CHORUSES (♩ = 280)

By Mark Sheafe, Clarence Robbins and Thornton Allen

Fine

SOLOS (on 7th chorus take 2nd ending)

11. Ballin' The Jack

PLAY 5 CHORUSES (♩ = 128)

By Jim Burris and Chris Smith

12. When The Saints Go Marchin' In

PLAY 12 CHORUSES (♩ = 254)

American Gospel Hymn

13. Who's Sorry Now?

PLAY 5 CHORUSES (♩ = 188)
CD Tracks 13 and 16

Words by Bert Kalmar and Harry Ruby
Music by Ted Snyder

14. China Boy

PLAY 7 CHORUSES (♩= 248)
CD Tracks 14 and 17

By Dick Winfree and Phil Boutelje

15. Toot, Toot, Tootsie! (Goodbye!)

PLAY 5 CHORUSES (♩= 240)
CD Tracks 15 and 18

Words and Music by Gus Kahn, Ernie Erdman,
Dan Russo, and Ted Fiorito

45

1. Down By The Riverside

PLAY 6 CHORUSES (♩ = 220)

American Gospel Song

2. Smiles

PLAY 5 CHORUSES (♩ = 160)

By J. Will Callahan and Lee S. Roberts

3. Jazz Me Blues

4. Wabash Blues

PLAY 3 CHORUSES (♩ = 106)

By Dave Ringle and Fred Meinken

SOLOS

ritard for ending – – ʼ

5. Ja-Da

PLAY 8 CHORUSES (♩= 174)

By Bob Carleton

Drum Intro

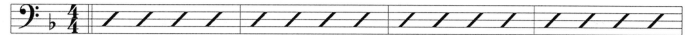

SOLOS

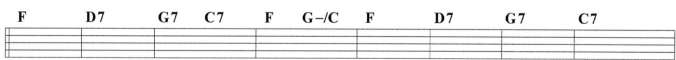

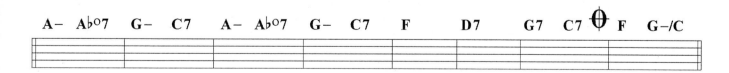

⊕ CODA

6. Avalon

PLAY 7 CHORUSES (♩ = 250)

By Al Jolson and B.G. DeSylva
Music by Vincent Rose

51

7. Just A Closer Walk With Thee

PLAY 4 CHORUSES (♩ = 66)

American Spiritual

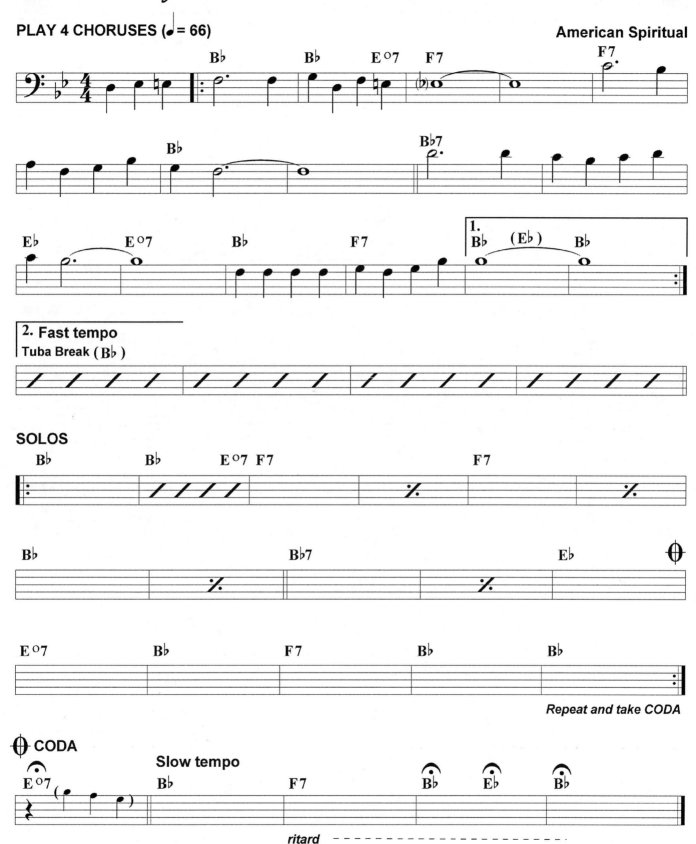

Repeat and take CODA

8. Some Of These Days

PLAY 6 CHORUSES (♩ = 212)

By Shelton Brooks

9. A Good Man Is Hard To Find

PLAY 4 CHORUSES (♩ = 112)

By Eddie Green

10. Washington and Lee Swing

PLAY 7 CHORUSES (♩ = 280)

By Mark Sheafe, Clarence Robbins and Thornton Allen

11. Ballin' The Jack

PLAY 5 CHORUSES (♩ = 128)   By Jim Burris and Chris Smith

12. When The Saints Go Marchin' In

PLAY 12 CHORUSES ($\quad$ = 254)

American Gospel Hymn

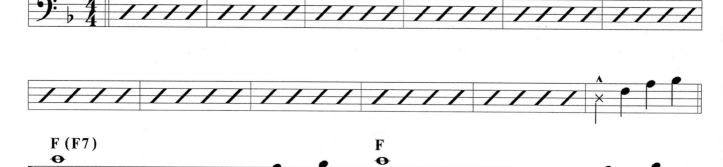

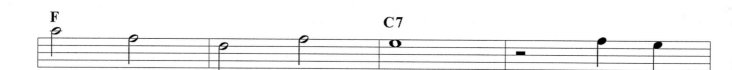

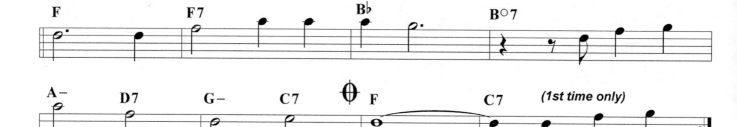

SOLOS

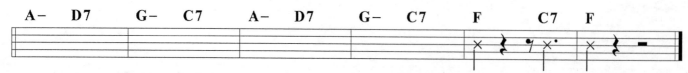

⊕**CODA**

A−	D7	G−	C7	A−	D7	G−	C7	F		C7	F

13. Who's Sorry Now?

PLAY 5 CHORUSES (♩ = 188)
CD Tracks 13 and 16

Words by Bert Kalmar and Harry Ruby
Music by Ted Snyder

14. China Boy

PLAY 7 CHORUSES (♩ = 248)
CD Tracks 14 and 17

By Dick Winfree and Phil Boutelje

15. Toot, Toot, Tootsie! (Goodbye!)

PLAY 5 CHORUSES ($\quad$ = 240)
CD Tracks 15 and 18

Words and Music by Gus Kahn, Ernie Erdman,
Dan Russo, and Ted Fiorito

Each Play-A-Long contains at least one stereo CD and a coordinated booklet with parts FOR ALL INSTRUMENTS. The volumes do not necessarily get progressively more difficult. Popularly termed *"The Most Widely-Used Improvisation Tools On The Market!"*

The special stereo separation technique is ideal for use by rhythm players.
The left channel includes bass and drums, while the right channel contains piano or guitar and drums.

"Anyone Can Improvise" by Jamey Aebersold
BEST-SELLING DVD ON JAZZ IMPROV!
2-HOUR DVD Featuring Jamey only $19.95

JAMEY'S SUGGESTED ORDER OF STUDY: Volumes 1, 24, 21, 116, 2, 54, 3, 70, 5, 84, etc. **Vol. 1 and 24 work to form a strong foundation.**

✔	VOL.#	TITLE	FORMAT	PRICE
	1	"JAZZ: HOW TO PLAY AND IMPROVISE"	BK/CD	15.90
	2	"NOTHIN' BUT BLUES"	BK/CD	15.90
	3	"THE II/V7/I PROGRESSION"	BK/2CDs	19.95
	4	"MOVIN' ON"	BK/CD	14.90
	5	"TIME TO PLAY MUSIC"	BK/CD	15.90
	6	CHARLIE PARKER - "ALL BIRD"	BK/CD	15.90
	7	MILES DAVIS	BK/CD	14.90
	8	SONNY ROLLINS	BK/CD	15.90
	9	WOODY SHAW	BK/CD	15.90
	10	DAVID BAKER - "EIGHT CLASSIC JAZZ ORIGINALS"	BK/CD	9.95
	11	HERBIE HANCOCK	BK/CD	15.90
	12	DUKE ELLINGTON	BK/CD	15.90
	13	CANNONBALL ADDERLEY	BK/CD	15.90
	14	BENNY GOLSON - "EIGHT JAZZ CLASSICS"	BK/CD	15.90
	15	"PAYIN' DUES"	BK/CD	15.90
	16	"TURNAROUNDS, CYCLES, & II/V7s"	BK/4CDs	19.95
	17	HORACE SILVER	BK/CD	15.90
	18	HORACE SILVER	BK/CD	15.90
	19	DAVID LIEBMAN	BK/CD	15.90
	20	JIMMY RANEY w/GUITAR	BK/CD	15.90
	21	"GETTIN' IT TOGETHER"	BK/2CDs	19.95
	22	"FAVORITE STANDARDS"	BK/2CDs	19.95
	23	"ONE DOZEN STANDARDS"	BK/2CDs	19.95
	24	"MAJOR & MINOR"	BK/2CDs	19.95
	25	"ALL-TIME STANDARDS"	BK/2CDs	19.95
	26	"THE SCALE SYLLABUS"	BK/2CDs	15.00
	27	JOHN COLTRANE	BK/CD	15.90
	28	JOHN COLTRANE	BK/CD	15.90
	29	"PLAY DUETS WITH JIMMY RANEY" w/GUITAR	BK/CD	14.90
	30A	"RHYTHM SECTION WORKOUT" - PIANO & GUITAR	BK/CD	14.90
	30B	"RHYTHM SECTION WORKOUT" - BASS & DRUMS	BK/CD	14.90
	31	"JAZZ BOSSA NOVAS"	BK/CD	15.90
	32	"BALLADS"	BK/CD	15.90
	33	WAYNE SHORTER	BK/2CDs	19.95
	34	"JAM SESSION"	BK/2CDs	19.95
	35	CEDAR WALTON	BK/CD	14.90
	36	"BEBOP AND BEYOND"	BK/CD	14.90
	37	SAMMY NESTICO	BK/CD	9.95
	38	"CLASSIC SONGS FROM THE BLUE NOTE JAZZ ERA"	BK/2CDs	19.95
	39	"SWING, SWING, SWING"	BK/CD	15.90
	40	"'ROUND MIDNIGHT"	BK/2CDs	19.95
	41	"BODY AND SOUL"	BK/2CDs	19.95
	42	"BLUES IN ALL KEYS"	BK/CD	15.90
	43	"GROOVIN' HIGH"	BK/CD	15.90
	44	"AUTUMN LEAVES"	BK/CD	15.90
	45	BILL EVANS	BK/CD	15.90
	46	"OUT OF THIS WORLD"	BK/CD	15.90
	47	"I GOT RHYTHM CHANGES" - IN ALL KEYS	BK/CD	15.90
	48	DUKE ELLINGTON - "IN A MELLOW TONE"	BK/CD	15.90
	49	"SUGAR" w/ORGAN	BK/CD	14.90
	50	MILES DAVIS - "THE MAGIC OF MILES"	BK/CD	15.90
	51	"NIGHT & DAY"	BK/CD	15.90
	52	"COLLECTOR'S ITEMS"	BK/CD	15.90
	54	"MAIDEN VOYAGE"	BK/CD	15.90
	55	JEROME KERN - "YESTERDAYS"	BK/CD	14.90
	56	THELONIOUS MONK	BK/CD	15.90
	57	"MINOR BLUES IN ALL KEYS"	BK/CD	15.90
	58	"UNFORGETTABLE STANDARDS"	BK/CD	14.90
	59	"INVITATION" w/ORGAN	BK/2CDs	19.95
	60	FREDDIE HUBBARD	BK/CD	15.90
	61	"BURNIN'"	BK/CD	15.90
	62	WES MONTGOMERY	BK/CD	14.90
	63	TOM HARRELL	BK/CD	14.90
	64	"SALSA, LATIN, JAZZ"	BK/CD	14.90
	65	"FOUR & MORE" w/ORGAN	BK/2CDs	19.95
	66	BILLY STRAYHORN - "LUSH LIFE"	BK/CD	15.90

✔	VOL.#	TITLE	FORMAT	PRICE
	67	"TUNE UP"	BK/CD	9.95
	68	"GIANT STEPS"	BK/CD	15.90
	69	CHARLIE PARKER - "BIRD GOES LATIN"	BK/CD	15.90
	70	"KILLER JOE"	BK/CD	15.90
	71	"EAST OF THE SUN"	BK/CD	15.90
	72	"STREET OF DREAMS"	BK/CD	15.90
	73	OLIVER NELSON - "STOLEN MOMENTS"	BK/CD	15.90
	74	"LATIN JAZZ"	BK/CD	15.90
	75	"COUNTDOWN TO GIANT STEPS"	BK/2CDs	19.95
	76	DAVID BAKER - "HOW TO LEARN TUNES"	BK/CD	19.95
	77	PAQUITO D'RIVERA	BK/CD	15.90
	78	"JAZZ HOLIDAY CLASSICS"	BK/CD	15.90
	79	"AVALON"	BK/CD	9.95
	80	"INDIANA"	BK/CD	9.95
	81	DAVID LIEBMAN - "STANDARDS & ORIGINALS"	BK/CD	9.95
	82	DEXTER GORDON	BK/CD	15.90
	83	THE BRECKER BROTHERS	BK/CD	16.90
	84	DOMINANT 7TH WORKOUT	BK/2CDs	19.95
	85	ANDY LAVERNE-"TUNES YOU THOUGHT YOU KNEW"	BK/CD	15.90
	86	HORACE SILVER - "SHOUTIN' OUT"	BK/CD	9.95
	87	BENNY CARTER - "WHEN LIGHTS ARE LOW"	BK/CD	9.95
	88	"MILLENNIUM BLUES"	BK/CD	9.95
	89	"DARN THAT DREAM"	BK/CD	15.90
	90	"ODD TIMES"	BK/CD	15.90
	91	"PLAYER'S CHOICE"	BK/CD	9.95
	92	LENNIE NIEHAUS	BK/CD	9.95
	93	"WHAT'S NEW?"	BK/CD	15.90
	94	"HOT HOUSE"	BK/CD	9.95
	95	"500 MILES HIGH"	BK/CD	15.90
	96	DAVE SAMUELS - "LATIN QUARTER"	BK/CD	15.90
	97	"STANDARDS WITH STRINGS"	BK/CD	16.90
	98	ANTONIO CARLOS JOBIM w/GUITAR	BK/CD	15.90
	99	TADD DAMERON - "SOULTRANE"	BK/CD	15.90
	100	"ST LOUIS BLUES" DIXIELAND	BK/CD	15.90
	101	ANDY LAVERNE - "SECRET OF THE ANDES"	BK/CD	15.90
	102	JERRY BERGONZI - "SOUND ADVICE"	BK/CD	9.95
	103	DAVID SANBORN	BK/CD	16.90
	104	KENNY WERNER - "FREE PLAY"	BK/CD	15.90
	105	DAVE BRUBECK - "IN YOUR OWN SWEET WAY"	BK/CD	15.90
	106	LEE MORGAN - "SIDEWINDER"	BK/CD	15.90
	107	"IT HAD TO BE YOU!" - STANDARDS FOR SINGERS	BK/2CDs	19.95
	108	JOE HENDERSON - "INNER URGE"	BK/CD	15.90
	109	DAN HAERLE - "FUSION"	BK/CD	15.90
	110	"WHEN I FALL IN LOVE" - ROMANTIC BALLADS	BK/CD	15.90
	111	JJ JOHNSON	BK/CD	15.90
	112	COLE PORTER - "21 GREAT STANDARDS"	BK/2CDs	19.95
	113	"EMBRACEABLE YOU" - BALLADS FOR ALL SINGERS	BK/2CDs	19.95
	114	"GOOD TIME"	BK/4CDs	19.95
	115	RON CARTER	BK/2CDs	16.90
	116	"MILES OF MODES" - MODAL JAZZ	BK/2CDs	19.95
	117	"COLE PORTER FOR SINGERS"	BK/2CDs	19.95
	118	JOEY DEFRANCESCO - "GROOVIN' JAZZ" w/ORGAN	BK/CD	15.90
	119	BOBBY WATSON	BK/CD	9.95
	120	"FEELIN' GOOD" - BLUES IN B-3 w/ORGAN	BK/CD	15.90
	121	PHIL WOODS	BK/CD	15.90
	122	JIMMY HEATH	BK/CD	15.90
	123	"NOW'S THE TIME" - JOEY DEFRANCESCO TRIO w/ORGAN	BK/CD	15.90
	124	"BRAZILIAN JAZZ"	BK/CD	15.90
	125	"CHRISTMAS CAROL CLASSICS"	BK/CD	16.90
	126	RANDY BRECKER w/RANDY BRECKER	BK/2CDs	19.95
	127	EDDIE HARRIS - "LISTEN HERE"	BK/CD	15.90
	128	DJANGO REINHARDT - "GYPSY JAZZ" w/GUITAR	BK/CD	15.90
	129	A JAZZY CHRISTMAS	BK/CD	16.90
	130	"PENNIES FROM HEAVEN"	BK/2CDs	19.95
	131	"CRY ME A RIVER"	BK/CD	16.90
	132	"ON THE STREET WHERE YOU LIVE"	BK/CD	16.90
	133	"DOWN BY THE RIVERSIDE" - DIXIELAND CLASSICS	BK/CD	16.90

All prices subject to change without notice. Visit www.jazzbooks.com for current pricing information.